# CHAOS THEORIES

# CHAOS THEORIES

## Elizabeth Hazen

Alan Squire Publishing
Bethesda, Maryland

Alan Squire Publishing

*Chaos Theories* is published by Alan Squire Publishing, an imprint of the Santa Fe Writers Project.

ISBN: 978-1-942892-02-1

Jacket design by Randy Stanard, Dewitt Designs, www.dewittdesigns.com.
Cover photo, "Pearl Piper," by William Lawrence, Hankins/Lawrence Images.
Inside jacket photo by Jessica Anya Blau.
Copy editing and interior design by Nita Congress.
Printing consultant: Steven Waxman.
Printed by R R Donnelley.

First Edition

*Ordo Vagorum*

# PRAISE FOR *CHAOS THEORIES*

In *Chaos Theories*, Elizabeth Hazen explores the "instabilities" of the human heart through the organizing impulses of poetry, which work to make sense, make order of memory, desire, and regret. This is a book of bodies and tongues but also of bright intellect, the mind scientific here, methodical and beautiful in its efforts "to narrate, fit events to plot."

— Jehanne Dubrow, author of *Home Front* and
*The Arranged Marriage*

Elizabeth Hazen finds speech for the mysteries and paradoxes of existence, speech she puts down in expertly cadenced lines that "produce the proper notes" of a restless imagination looking to find the "absent whole" in human experience.

— Michael Collier, Director, The Bread Loaf Writers'
Conference, author of *An Individual History* and
*Dark Wild Realm*

In *Chaos Theories*, time haunts us with decisions and memories, but time also reveals the world's recursive wonders, if we can only look and listen as Hazen teaches us to do.

— Dora Malech, author of *Say So* and
*Shore Ordered Ocean*

# ACKNOWLEDGMENTS

To the editors at Alan Squire Publishing, Rose Solari and James Patterson, I owe my deepest gratitude. Thank you for believing in my writing and for working so hard to make this book happen. Thanks also to Andrew Gifford and the team at Santa Fe Writers Project for your guidance and support, and to Nita Congress and Randy Stanard for your help with the book's design.

Jessica Blau, Betsy Boyd, Elisabeth Dahl, Jane Delury, Carl Ehrhardt, Kathy Flann, Martin Galvin, Paris Goudas, Rosie Goudas, Christine Grillo, James Magruder, Chrissi Moore, Marion Winik, and Sarah Woodruff — without your feedback, your encouragement, and your friendship, this book would not exist. Thank you.

Robert, Margaret, and Benjamin Hazen — thank you for the opportunities, inspiration, solace, and love you have always provided.

And Patrick Flynn Eckenrode — so many of these poems are for you. I wish you were here to read them.

I would like to acknowledge the following publications in which these poems first appeared:

*Arch*: "Summer 1985"

*Bellevue Literary Review*: "After Electro-Convulsive Therapy"

*Best American Poetry 2013, Southwest Review*: "Thanatosis"

*Bluestem*: "Remains"

*Booth*: "Maxwell's Demon"

*The Common*: "Burial at Shanidar," "While our father is hunting rocks"

*The Common Online*: "Erosion," "Meditation on Divorce During Summer Storm," "Spring Planting"

*The Comstock Review*: "Bed Rest"

*Crab Orchard Review*: "Burning Trash"

*Fourteen Hills*: "Underwear Girl"

*Free State Review*: "Snapshots"

*Gargoyle*: "Coastal," "Ghost Story"

*Memoir Journal*: "Road Trip," "Winter Funeral"

*The Normal School*: "Chaos Theory," "Separation"

*The Nervous Breakdown*: "Closet"

*PANK*: "Bottom Dwellers," "Chaos Theory," "Physics Lesson," "Separation"

*Salamander*: "Bottom Dwellers," "Physics Lesson"

*Signature Journal*: "Shark Teeth"

*The Threepenny Review*: "Trilobites"

*Three Quarter Review*: "First Word in a Time of Mourning"

*The Toronto Quarterly*: "Extraction," "Meditation on Entropy"

*Unsplendid*: "Last Anniversary," "The Spectroscope"

*Urbanite*: "Skin"

*for Gregory Flynn Ehrhardt*

Above all, in a universe ruled by entropy, drawing inexorably toward greater and greater disorder, how does order arise?

James Gleick, *Chaos*

# CONTENTS

# III

I

# CHAOS THEORY

You'd think disorder, anarchy, but chaotic
systems twist into something like control:
patterns algorithmic, self-replicating,

infinite. All it takes for things to turn
is a blip, a shift minute as the flutter of wings,
the opening of a door, a telephone

unanswered, the clap of voices shouting *Wait!*
My rage comes out of nowhere — the glass explodes
when it hits the wall, as physics says it must,

but who knew I was capable of this?
I wake each day to an alarm. Each night
I watch the neon time tick by. A person

can disappear from this equation, swift
as the click of a pawnshop trigger. The effect
is vast as tectonic shifts, mountains spewing

ash clouds, a newborn's blue-faced breath, but how
can we isolate the cause of his departure?
Chaos gives us endless bifurcations,

the path of time from next to next, no chance
of turning back. Instabilities overwhelm
the Earth: addiction, population growth,

disease, storms, earthquakes, infidelities,
and a simple pendulum with its routine
*tick-tock, tick-tock.* Even this sorry heart,

aperiodic after all, pounds wildly
at entrances, exits, the memory of his touch,
try as it will to keep a steady beat.

# SHARK TEETH

In the beginning, I strolled for an hour or two,
picking up pieces that flickered black, learning
to ignore the tricky chips of mussel shell
that most mistake for teeth. My pockets held
entire mouths, and soon I saw nothing

but their shimmer through the silt. Back home I sorted
great white, mako, tiger, snaggletooth: stacks
of trays filled with teeth, disembodied, mismatched,
shiny black and blue. I thumbed serrated edges,
stroked the squared-off roots, counted what was missing.

I bought hip waders and braved high tide, filling
my pack with shark teeth, skate teeth, hunks of whale bone.
Soon I disappeared for days, returning soaked
and weighted down. There is no end to this searching:
a single shark can shed ten thousand teeth

or more; its grace is regeneration: new teeth
fill in the gaps; the lost ones fall to the sea floor,
fossilize, emerge again with the turning
of tide: rogue pieces of an absent whole,
sharp echoes of a story I once knew.

# WINTER FUNERAL

The embouchure opens to the unknown
of ocean, the horizon's deceptive line.

It unfolds to plain, the lowest point
rising to action, unraveling grasses,

dirt, invisible distance. It presses
an estuary of breath through pursed lips,

tensed cheek and jaw, a practiced tongue.
We have heard this all before. One needs

structure to produce the proper notes.
Cold intensifies error. My father

clasps his trumpet in his coat, warms up
the muscles in his face. Valves can only

do so much. Even the heart, pumping
faithfully, grows tired, but no note breaks,

no rest lingers in this space between breath
and music, this plot and what comes next.

# GHOST STORY

Your tongue, when loose, spills secrets you have held
for years, but memory distorts. What you heard

is not the same as what was said; what you saw
is not what you first believed: catastrophe

of a child's tears, the monster's face at the window.
You have deadbolts on all your doors, but ghosts

can move through walls, inhabit your skin, reflect
like wavelengths, echoing light or sound, the idea

but not the thing: intention, promise, fable,
even who you are today, so certain

of what you will and will not do. That ghost
is watching you unscrew the bottle, pour

three fingers, four. You tell yourself there's nothing
to fear, nothing can hurt you here. Ghosts are

not real; they are echoes, illusions, tricks of ears
and eyes; they have no skin, no fingernails.

The voice you hear is in your head. Over
and over she asks, *Then why are you afraid?*

# HIS NAME HERE

## 1.

For years you let the morning light burn
through the smoke that gave your breath
dimension,

that puffed up your words,
arrogant parrots making claims.

Months went by, seasons passed.
The light shifted

and something caught you:
the vibration of your own laughter, a shouting man outside.
On the periphery,

a shadow in the doorway:
someone leaving and not coming back,

the echo of a gunshot you did not hear.

# 2.

Now, curtains drawn, night comes like lights
darkening in a theater.

Your body unsettles.

The doctor showed you. You saw his face,
his bones bright white
against the black of your insides.

You sleep deeply, but dream of children born without faces,
whole houses crumbling at your touch, boils blistering on
    your skin,
rooms without windows or doors.

# 3.

Silence is the air you breathe.
The word unspoken is a name
hanging heavy as wet clothes on the line.

A body moves inside a body.

Ashes settle in another country.

Your body is full to bursting. There is no room for grief:
a body breaking out of a body, demanding space —

how can ashes take so much space? —

and a single breath to name him.

# GIRLS AT THE BUS DEPOT

There are alleyways, of course, and underground
garages at the bus depot. Passengers

come and go, and girls stand by the benches, smoking
Reds, pretending to be bored. The men cannot

believe how girls so young can fill a pair
of jeans like that. And you cannot believe

yourself as you accept a grown man's tongue
thick with malt liquor, so hungry are you

for his approval. You go all the way
down to P5 where he says no one will find you.

Some of these men have daughters your same age.
Some have bulges in their pants to which they direct

your hands, sometimes gently, but more often with
pressure that you cannot resist. Gray concrete

smell of gasoline and urine will haunt
your dreams for years. Engines rev, disaster

holds its breath — and no matter what you tell
yourself tonight, no matter what you tell

yourself in twenty years, you are still there,
terrified, alone, still waiting for someone

to tell you *Stop! Come home!* Back home, you tell
stories about missed connections and dead

batteries. You learn the art of secrets: rinse
your mouth with mouthwash, scrub and scrub your hands.

# BED REST

## I.

I never knew what violence it takes to fill
the cracks; the rain had been spilling

in for months, our walls weeping, our ceiling
like papier-mâché, damp globs falling

to the floor. Now weather is without and the men
work to keep it there, mending

the spaces that let the outside in. Roofing hatchets,
slate rippers, wrecking bars: the racket

of their grunting fraternity keeps me awake until
one man's cell rings and he tells

the others to take five. I know the woman
who has called: her voice is like a chisel; she wants

answers. *No*, says the roofer, he doesn't see that other
woman anymore; that other

woman is a slut and a liar. *Yes*, he loves you.
*Yes*, he'll call later. *Yes!* He wouldn't say it if it wasn't true.

# II.

The men hammer at the cracks until they give, until
the broken pieces fall away and all

that's left is space for them to fill with something else.
There is no space left inside me; there is only this

time, this bed, this body like a house, this telephone
that does not ring, this noise above me like a playground
    song

no one teaches silly girls. And inside me
a fist clenching, someone waiting to break free.

# UNDERWEAR GIRL

The way, in movies, people move through ghosts,
you power straight through me, Underwear Girl,

trailing mascara in cartoon swirls,
your cotton panties pink as bubblegum.

A boy in a muscle shirt chases you. *Come back!*
He is young, embarrassed, maybe in love with you,

maybe just in love with the way your body
moves — all passion and mystery and control.

Behind him, a woman waves a pair of pants,
crying, *Wait! Don't go!* How they all want you,

Underwear Girl! I know your fury feels
too big for clothes. No pair of designer jeans

could ever contain your rage; you think if you keep
running, it means you will arrive somewhere.

I want you to be right, but I know what burns
you up inside, and that fire can't keep you warm.

It is November. Your feet are turning blue.
Underwear Girl, you can't stop time or cellulite

or regret, can't deny entropy, elastic
waistbands, tedium. Those who play chase now

will fall back, give up, pursue other ambitions
on other streets, and what will you do with your rage then,

Underwear Girl? Will you squeeze it into control-
top pantyhose, swallow it like benzos,

take it out on a husband who never saw it coming?
Underwear Girl, my thighs once looked like that,

toned and tensed to fight the forces of evil.
We all rage against something, feel pressed for time

and money, exit strategies. No one
can run forever. Underwear Girl, there are things

you may not understand yet. If you would just
see me, I could tell you so many things.

# COASTAL

Our mothers' beaches were East Coast, brown and blurry,
like slow-shuttered photographs or the view

from a moving train. They spread blankets, unloaded
buckets, sieves, shovels. They cranked umbrellas,

settled in, adjusting their suits, slathered
our backs with lotion, told us *Go on, play.*

When they took their eyes off us it was to watch
a seagull pick over crustaceous remains

or to rest their eyes, the insides of their lids
glowing bright then darkening with the passing clouds.

Seldom did they get wet except to edge
their toes to surf or trickle fists of water

down the fronts of their bright red suits. Lipsticked,
even at the beach, these mothers, masked strangers,

barked commands, their fleshy embraces vast
softness that buried us, birthed us, sent us

inevitably away from them, toward water.
Later there were translucent promises

on the glossy fronts of postcards sent from friends
we barely knew, showing aqua-backed schools

of fish, bright as hard candy, slick and unafraid.
These images were dreams that fell as hard

as stupor after a night of heavy drinking.
In my mouth the names of these beaches catch

like lies — Rhodes, Ipanema, Negril —
and all the while my son moves toward me across

a coast of hungry rocks. This ocean is
a mercy, a mouth, a way out of this ragged earth

that claws us down, this broken promise of land
waiting to swallow us whole, hold us deep

and speechless: memories, secrets, shipwrecks, gold
coins glittering at the bottom of a sea.

# FIRST WORD IN A TIME OF MOURNING

I told myself clouds, but stars confronted me,
my cosmic ignorance: speed of light,

gravity, the workings of clocks, cell division,
fossilization, my skin's elasticity,

and some nights the lunar phase that leaves no moon
to find. I carried you in circles,

eyes angling for crescent, quarter, halo.
You pursed your lips, waited for my revelation.

If absence could be filled at will, disappointment
swept away like ash — if negative spaces

did not call us here, to shadow — if all it took
was gesture, words — but I cannot shift

the geometry of space. I have no answers
to give you. I have held on tightly only to find

my palm impressed with fingernails: parentheses
waiting for content. Should I say, *Look there,*

*little one! Heaven, empty as a drained pool?*
Forgive me. I met your first effort at speech

with silence, the only answer consonant
with loss, my offering: this blank sky.

# EXTRACTION

My milk ripe with Percocet, I let
my son wail through the night, coming back,

at last, to the isolation of my body,
the distinction of my flesh; I break space

to move along. The maxillary molars
stay undisturbed: *Better if we leave well*

*enough alone.* Such is wisdom: idle till
that spark of pain. I tongue the clot. Soon tissue

will fill in the gap and harden. Across the hall
my son cuts teeth, gnaws his knuckles, but stops short

of breaking skin. A body holds more mysteries
than the mouth can bring itself to speak. Soon

my breasts will unswell; the pain of weaning
will fade away; the pain in my gum will fade

away: already the socket is closing. One day
my son's mouth will bloom with teeth, then questions,

secrets. Even now I hear slamming doors,
revving departures, the spaces left behind.

# BURIAL AT SHANIDAR

*Pollen found in one of the Shanidar graves suggests that
Neanderthals, too, buried flowers with their dead.*

The pollen could be mere coincidence —
traces left by a prehistoric rat
that ate flowers near the grave — but we prefer

believing cavemen buried blossoms there.
See the bereaved weeping? Over foothills
she lumbers. Mammoths trumpet in the distance.

All flowers were wild then. Grape hyacinth,
cornflower, hollyhock. She gathers armfuls,
asking *Why?* She lays the bouquet on his chest,

closes him into the cave floor. Perhaps
she says a prayer. See? Even from this distance
we dream of gardens where there should be stone.

# SPRING PLANTING

If not the wind, still something carries
everything away. Just this morning
my son and I threw apple seeds

to grass. He spoke of trees, but how
much stays in one place long enough
to root itself? How much blossoms,

after all? Dandelion fluff,
memory of a face: our beginnings
are just a cry for breath, our ends

are but a sigh. And always something
falls short of expectations. Cause
and effect are everything. I warned him

of birds, shadow, drought. Already
the predicament of risk plagues him.
We know nothing of what will happen, even

less of who we are. He asks
before he falls asleep, *What is God?*
This word I never thought to teach him.

He waits, and I think to myself:
*I opened my eyes to see; I opened
my mouth* — You know how this story ends.

# CERES

"Gravitational perturbations from Jupiter billions of years
ago prevented [Ceres] from becoming a full-fledged planet.
Ceres ended up among the leftover debris of planetary
formation in the main asteroid belt between Mars and
Jupiter." – NASA

In one version of the story Jupiter,
virile god of sky and thunder, is to blame
for her limitations, his gravitational pull
enough to stultify her growth. Her lesser
form, sculpted by impacts, obeys the dictates
of his belt – it's true – but let us not forget
her domain: growth, harvest, motherly love,

and like all mothers she is volatile, fierce,
instinctive. She is no mere passenger.
At any moment, she could decide to leave
her orbit, come raining down on us, blooming
apocalypse, so scientists punch numbers,
keep her in check, as if they could stop
her coming. Fools. She may be invisible,

even in the brightest light, but I can see
her burning from a hundred million miles
away; who cares if the calculations don't
bear this out? Let me tell you something about
the bearing out of things: when he pushed through me,
gagging for that first breath, no equation could
contain his need, my relief, the bleeding. And when

my heart rate dropped, I might have disappeared —
a star burning out, an asteroid imploding,
substance transforming to debris — but I wanted
only to sleep, wake up again, and feed
my son. From the moment we are born, gravity
presses down on us. We fight to lift our heads.
We bear hunger, secrets, the passage of time,

the limitations of our bodies, the knowledge
of what we almost were, and of what we are.
Oh, Ceres, I am not afraid of you.
You were not made for destruction, and however
the universe has failed you, you endure,
vivid in darkness, indefinable.
You are exactly where you want to be.

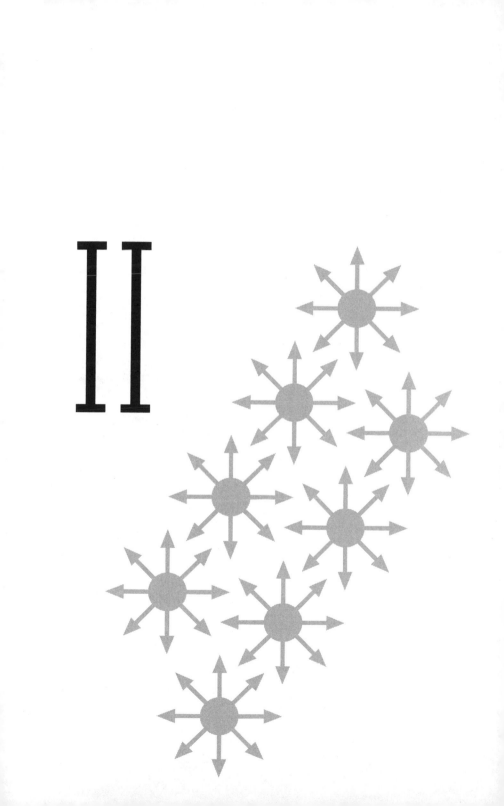

II

# STRANGE ATTRACTOR

One can't predict what happens next, yet even
chaos breeds patterns of a sort: sly singles

at the bar, nocturnal creatures stalking shadows,
cars cruising for motion's sake. I'm speaking out

of turn again. We all are sensitive
to first impressions, but initial conditions

shift swiftly and with little impetus.
I found him digging ditches in summer heat,

and soon we'd made declarations, smiled broadly
for photographs. It wasn't meant to be

a game, but I am strange and turbulent.
I move from this to that and this again —

always this again. Strange attractor, shifting
my gaze, on edge, plotting my next move. Movement

is a theory too — remember what the teacher
told us? Physics says we will keep moving,

though this can't be progress. More often we
spin circles, noting views that barely change.

I want my windows to reveal the world
unblurred, I want to understand the need

for headway, but all this motion has a way
of running things together. Who we are

has slipped from us again, slick fish refusing
stasis, our stubborn will to carry on.

# THANATOSIS

For those who cannot camouflage themselves,
the alternative to fight or flight is tonic
immobility. The victim's one trick:
to keel over. The cooling skin expels

foul smells, teeth clench, eyes glaze, the heart sustains
a sluggish thump. What's outside can't revive
the creature; it feels nothing, though alive,
paralyzed while the predator remains.

Waiting in the closet behind my mother's
dresses, scent of hyacinth, I transmute —
mouth pressed in the wool of her one good suit —
into a speechless, frozen thing. The others

call me from far away, but I am fixed
right here. As if these shadows have cast doubt
across my way of seeing, I don't want out,
and like the prey who plays at rigor mortis,

biding her time when the enemy is near,
while I'm inside this darkness I can see
no difference between death and immobility,
what it is to hide and to disappear.

# TRILOBITES

Before you understood the risk of breaking
things apart, you sat beside your father
in the quarry, mimicked the deft slipping
of his chisel between layers of shale;
before you had the threat of time holding
you, the arms of your child holding you,
the voice on the phone, *Hold on* — there was the quarry,
the heft of stones in your cupped hands, the grace

of chisel, hammer, pick. You learned patience,
opening rock after rock, finding clusters
of brachiopods, fragments of thorax, or nothing
but smooth gray shale — and sometimes a trilobite
intact, spiny, armored, its twin halves fat
as big toes. Then he would set his chisel down,
cradle the find, lick dust from its two faces.
He dug through outcrops, gravel pits, creek beds,

searching for that reflected face, as yours
hardened. What did he seek in them? They warp
his shelves with prehistoric weight. You see
nothing except the charcoal blotches left
behind, that old stone pit, the mirroring,
the dust — no human quality save the way,
if you squint, they resemble mouths — the round
darkness, the black O waiting to shape speech.

# ROAD TRIP

It began, as most stories do, with a mistake:
a squirrel caught under the tread, smeared across
the road like viscous paint. When it happened again
the man could not be sure if he'd intended
to accelerate, but soon he was hungry for blood,

bone, entrails, raging down the highway
for raccoons, stray cats — you can see where this is going —
a neighbor's terrier, a golden lab.
The story ended with implication: a woman
on the sidewalk watering roses, the man's

maniacal grin. Our father hammed it up,
slurping sibilant passages about oozing
canine corpses, pausing for effect, flourishing
the flashlight beneath his bearded face.
Our mother gasped, manufactured fear, but we

could not contain our laughter. The campground
calm, except for the frenetic buzz of insects,
our father's voice. Later, zipped in our separate
tent, roots gouging our spines, the rustle of our parents'
sleeping bag, their heavy breathing, the moon's light

enough to shape shadows that dart up
the canvas walls. In the morning, our father,
restored to stoic silence, hits the gas.
Buckled in the backseat, landscape scrolling,
we watch the world undone with distance, speed.

# BURNING TRASH

Boys start fires all the time — it's a rite
of passage — so when your father gives you the task
of setting fire to the family's trash,
you don't mind, and when the flames ignite

inside the old dishwasher he heaved
into the woods behind the house, you smoke
a cigarette, glancing up the path, and stoke
the flames with a stick. Above you sneaky leaves

let through a glimpse of tomorrow, but today
is still consumed with the past: yesterday's news,
junk mail, cardboard boxes, empty bottles. The fumes
of crackling plastic make you sick, but you stay

until the fire reduces the week to ash.
You're a little let down that the fire doesn't last,
doesn't leap from the dishwasher, spreading past
the forest's edge. All that burns is trash.

My love, be patient — you who are so taken
by the promise of destruction, so watchful
for what lies beyond your father's woods: the pull
of the future like a girl waiting, naked

and certain. It is time for you to learn:
not all fires can be contained, not all traces
of the things we throw away can be erased
with a single match, and even as you yearn

for new fire to burn a path away from here,
the old flames smolder, and the steely walls
buckle, and from the distance your father calls
you back. His voice grows louder every year.

# DOMESTIC NUDE 11

*After the photograph by Helmut Newton*

It could be any nobody's backyard,
the way the concrete squares, carelessly placed,
construct a rutted walkway to the woodpile —
and the pile itself, so vast, runs off the page,
posing a risk simply because its surface
threatens to chafe and splinter my pretty skin —

or rather *hers*, which is a model's skin,
smooth and unscarred. She makes the simple yard
an Eden of sorts, a masterpiece. The surface
of the photograph — though flat — seems in places
to rise from the two dimensions of the page:
her glowing white stiletto, the climbing pile,

her breasts, the rotting log she took from the pile
and holds, cocked like a gun, against her skin.
An offshoot points to the focus of the page:
between her legs, darkly shadowed like the yard.
Though you seek mystery in these hidden places,
they are as ordinary as the surface

of the dusty ground on which she stands. She faces
you with disdain, protective of the woodpile.
As far as you can see, she never places
her burden back on the stack or sweeps her skin
clean of dirt or leaves. She stays in the backyard,
a constant soldier committed to the page.

Her accusing eyes, hair closing like a page
over her face, the threat of all those surfaces:
a chain-link fence, jagged bark, the grassless yard.
I want to throw her body on the pile,
paint her with gasoline, set fire to her skin —
but I have come from the same places:

I too stand naked, tricking my dark places
into deeper shadow. I live inside a page,
kindling for future fires. My sagging skin,
my burning domesticity: this surface
a collage of practiced gestures I compile
to mask the fury of my own backyard.

# CLOSET

The hallway to your father's closet lengthens
as in a horror flick, and already breathless

at the threshold, you inhale the musky-raw
smells of tweed and leather that will settle

in your hair, so hours later you will think
of the closet, of the photos in the magazines

hidden on his sweater shelf — the lighting
in these pictures, orangey-pink, suggesting flesh

and places deep inside the body that you
have not yet found. The women — spreading wide,

splaying endless legs across the page
like fleshy insects, turning themselves inside out,

bodies spilling secrets — they compel you
to flip to less distressing images of breasts

and hands, flicking tongues. You skim their interests:
*Vanessa likes kung fu. Brandi studies*

*the stars.* You want eyes that prowl like that, dreams
worthy of print, and lingerie that serves no purpose

but to accentuate the perfect nakedness
you still believe all girls grow into — but

these women do not see you, just as you
do not see them, do not see yourself: your eyes

are closed. You disappear behind your father's
flannel suits, and when you emerge from the closet,

flushed and reeling, no one has noticed you
were gone; the world remains unchanged, though lingering

on the tip of your tongue, a word takes shape
like the answer to a question no one has asked you yet.

# AFTER ELECTRO-CONVULSIVE THERAPY

Quiet fills the room
except for the spoon she clinks
                        and the rain
                                that plops
                in the lobster pot
        we placed
                        to catch the leak.

Purple lightning flashes.
                        Branches crack.
The electricity flickers and goes out.
                                The lobster pot flows over,
        onto the cold white floor.
                        She closes her eyes.
Rain continues to pour inside
                                and the pot overflows
                like the backyard stream
after the hurricane
                        that summer
I was seven,
        when we found a dog,
dead for weeks,
                washed up in the creek bed.

My father boiled the bones.
The grit and muscle cooked away
and we put it back together
piece by piece.

When we were done
nothing remained of it
but a skeleton clicking on its string
and the deep empty sockets
where its eyes should have been.

And she —
she closes her eyes.
Rain continues to pour inside.
The pot still overflows.
There is a darkness in this room. Her face alone
stands out, calm
and pale as bone.

# SUMMER 1985

*for my brother*

We blew our allowances on toy soldiers
and disc guns, spent mornings on the patio
before the air thickened, posing
the green figures in an offensive line
along the flagstones, the flower boxes, the picnic table.

Fast fingers topple men like dominoes,
so we took our time. Inside our mother tuned out
radio reports of hijackings and deficits.
She stacked the breakfast dishes in a daze
until a ringing phone, a lawnmower's growl,

our voices through the screen snapped her
to attention. She clapped, fake-ecstatic, distracted,
day bearing down like the memory
of an argument, the impossibility of keeping anything
in its place, these minutes gone, these years.

The color rising just beneath the surface
of her skin could have passed for sunburn, fever,
but even children understand the way
some things get buried, some things never
find release. On three, we unloaded our pistols,

swirling the air with colored discs spit out
like wads of gum. After, we gathered wreckage —
the toppled corpses and discharged rounds — as if
this game of war could win for her a battle
she seemed, in silence, always to be fighting.

# WHILE OUR FATHER IS HUNTING ROCKS

Mountains rise beyond the laundromat
like ocher waves about to crash; our father,
armed with tools and pack, tracks the rocks

without a map. Here, the laundromat is all
in a strip of vacancies; for miles, nothing
but dirt, dust, outcrop, sky. Our mother gives

us coins to clink in the machine; it gushes
cold, foams with the flower-scented soap we dump
from a plastic scoop. Out back, we kick the dirt:

curled in sagebrush, the carcass of a cat.
Inside, our mother's lost in swirls of fading
color, while somewhere in the rocks that look

so near collapse, our father carves out meaning.
When he returns to us, hours later, or days,
he pulls trilobites from his pack and licks them clean.

*See?* he says, and we do. Dusk hovering,
we chatter at him, showing him the laundry
we have helped our mother fold. At last, we lead him

to the cat, our great find, its stench rising, the novelty
of death a little less under his studied gaze,
and the flies buzzing like static, eager to feed.

# THE SPECTROSCOPE

Two toilet paper rolls shellacked to pipe,
fluorescent bulb, foil, a square of lined
plastic diffracting light: the spectroscope
transforms thin air into rainbow, its power
magical as endless handkerchiefs, rabbits
pulled from empty hats, women sawed in two.

My father said this radiance was photons,
wavelengths, quantum fingerprints, white light
broken into frequencies. These mechanics,
obscure as a magician's thread, escaped me,
but still I palmed the swath of rainbow, strummed
the glowing spectral lines. When he flipped off

the switch and left, I marveled at the air
around the spectroscope, the vacancy
still echoing light, as an empty cage still hums
with birdsong when the sheet is whisked away,
or a room holds the vibration of a voice,
a person's scent, long after he has gone.

# WHEN I WAS A GIRL

My memory is a haunted house that will
not let me leave. For miles rooftops

slant like disapproving brows. The house
is like a dollhouse, something make-believe,

but my eyelashes don't have that girlish curl,
my eyes don't shut when I lie down or roll

with glassy resignation. I haven't worn
a frock in years. In short, I disappoint.

My memory is a ghost who riffles through my drawers,
a menace who reads my diary and watches

me undress in hopes of finding evidence
to prove I'm nothing but a neatly folded lie.

My memory is a jealous girl who locks
me in this upstairs room. I think I hear

her leave, but she's a tricky bitch who returns
to keep me trapped right here. Her smile is

my smile, sweet as an Easter basket, filled
with useless trinkets, secrets that need no keeping.

My memory is the field on which I set
my sights, but distances undo me; my eyes

are hypocrites, my metaphors unsorted.
I rearrange the furniture. What else can I do?

My memory wants to tell a better story
in which I don't apologize for taking space.

I wear bright lipstick, musky scents. I smile,
tell him I am someone to be reckoned with.

# III

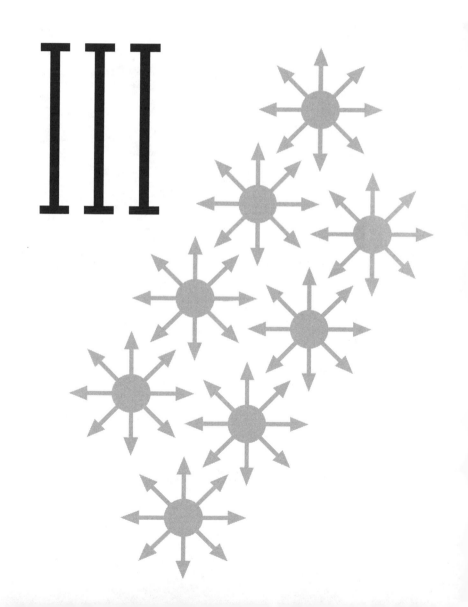

# MEDITATION ON ENTROPY

Tectonic plates are obvious shifters, still more
is moving here. The sea erodes the shoreline,
but that isn't what I mean. Consider grass,

the way its roots alone must hold the yard
in place, or the junk-filled creek bed drying up.
The dying fire. Time moves in one direction.

My son deploys toy soldiers. He's missing
two front teeth. My worry lines will deepen,
my nose expand; if I live long enough

I will have someone else's face — already
I don't know myself. Living, a constant
conversion, is confounded by this measuring.

In the Earth's core, nuclei of radioactive
elements decay. What I mean to say
is this: instability prevails. Last week

I missed the exit home, but I drove on
for miles in the wrong direction. Last
year I left my husband without warning.

One could say I'm not myself, but I've
been someone else before, and who's to judge
if she was better? This is what I know:

energy turns to heat that seeps toward surfaces.
Thermodynamics dictate that destruction
keeps us warm. I did what I had to do.

Death is indiscriminate, as you know
already: the living make the same mistakes,
the departed turn in their graves. Nightmares wrack

my son, but the static of my bad dreams
corrupts the standard line: *You're safe*, I lie
to soothe his fears. *Nothing can hurt you here.*

# SNAPSHOTS

The Earth tallies our losses: abacus
of ancient bone emerges out of rock,

layers of snow compress deep in glacial lakes:
blank blue ledger, millennia of falling.

Even now fault lines fracture canyons, gouges
like scores in a bedpost. So much passage

is documentation, our need for proof
and percentages. Objects left behind

are evidence, though of what we can't be sure:
receipts forgotten in a pocket; letters

pressed in books; empty vials stashed in drawers.
Consider how the tide's turning rearranges

everything. In a stack of blurry pasts I count
his faces, none as I remember it.

# PHYSICS LESSON

Response to force defines the mass of things:
a door defies a shoulder's thrust; a floor

fractures a dropped glass; fingertips submit
to paring knives; and all around you bodies

collapse like compact stars. Radiance defines
location, texture, shape: fleck of ash,

bone, sinew, grain of pine, the ligature
of meadow grass, the trajectory of stars.

Experts agree, whole galaxies are moving
in reverse, redshifting toward lower frequencies.

Why should this surprise you? Taillights glow
like red dwarf stars on the highway out of town.

Anonymous rooms conceal dark matter. Someone
withdraws into a vacuum, breathes the variegated

absences, the listless dawn. He is there,
propped on the edge of a rented bed. All systems

tend toward disorder, but look at his shoes,
regimented beside the locked door. You want

to show him something, but he draws the blinds,
angles them down. When he is gone, you will cling

to science: the emergent properties
of bad weather, quantum mechanics, black holes:

the promise that what you cannot see still lies,
waiting, somewhere just beyond your grasp.

# SEPARATION

Frog dissection teaches connectivity:
the eyes, blank globes, dangle nerves and muscles;

the heart, now hard as an eraser, once
pumped blood; but a shaky hand and scalpel don't

define division. Much less is required
to take a thing apart. My body, too,

divides itself, a measure to protect.
The inside is my secret, the outside

a lovely myth. I reach up, but nothing holds;
there is no leverage in the sky. The process

by which we come to understand our place
is lonely work. Like the specimen, incised,

pinned open, we watched ourselves undone. I made
the first cut, clamped down on your lungs, insisted,

*Take a breath.* I saw that you were falling,
feared the worst, but the Earth caught you, held you

sound, even as it spun, reconfiguring
itself, losing ground each day, its former

state displayed on maps covering the walls
that once held us together. How we dreamt

of travel, our precious world spread flat, tacked
in place, and always under our control.

# REMAINS

Disaster breeds new bones: a stegosaurus's
dorsal plates cut the earth like teeth; the excavated

creature reemerges, clamped together
in an echoing hall. The victims at Pompeii

prove the resilience of bone: the pyroclastic
blast left their skeletons intact. In mass graves

soldiers uncover trenches filled with bones
embracing bones, refusing to let go.

An overcrowded cemetery finds space
when flesh has gone, the consolidated bones

boxed in vaults. We all have bones to pick:
breath catching in our throats, a ringing telephone,

blinking highways, one last drink, a misplaced piece
of paper, a broken window, a name. A body

takes three hours to burn, more or less; the bones
become like gravel. In its mother's womb,

the child's bones are rubber; birth, its own disaster,
hardens the bones; they strengthen, sometimes break,

then heal, and years later grow brittle like the bones
of birds, hollow as stalks. Soon we move like puppets;

we take supplements; our bones buckle and we shrink.
Then just standing becomes a risk, and turning

back enough to snap a neck, yet still we look
for explanations. The earth brims with our remains,

so we dig for the pieces that will make us whole,
forgetting that bone is speechless, reveals nothing.

# FINAL THEORY

Our expectation is a sphere, the perfect
alignment of mouth and eyes, a Rorschach blot,
a butterfly, but symmetry is not
merely reflection. Throughout nature objects

skew, land erodes, our memories are a jumble,
yet there is symmetry in repetition:
stars, pixels, sleeplessness, the apparition
of his face like headlights in a tunnel.

Scientists claim universal symmetry,
say a "theory of everything" exists,
order, in spite of evidence, persists:
to know the mind of God, patterns are the key.

Prayer has symmetry, and funeral processions,
blood spatter, scattered ashes, a child's weeping,
cardboard boxes hidden for safekeeping,
his infinite silence, my unanswered questions.

# EROSION

A house perched on a cliff is static, but water
percolates inside the rock, sediment runs off,

the gradient steepens. The risk of falling deepens
as storms strip land, exposing roots and skeletons

of whale. Miles out, the ships that sever water
from sky know nothing of lost ground. Inside

a man considers walling off the rooms
that flank the looming edge, a sacrifice

like amputation, but instead he transplants
the house, losing only the foundation.

He uses steel beams and hydraulic jacks
to shift the structure back. The Earth, of course,

keeps spinning, space keeps filling in the gaps.
A million things can chip away at us,

breaking down that which we strive to keep intact:
mass wasting, surface creep, earthquakes, pounding waves.

There is no cure for time or stormy weather.
Even now, spring gales beat down the cliff's face.

Even now the man calculates his losses,
this trick of geometry, the distance left,

as if the right angle truly buys more time,
and solid ground itself could be enough.

# SKIN

## 1.

Spread out, my skin is as big as a bed, this organ
breathing through every pore — flinch, constrict, recoil,
    burn —
and just beneath my skin, the vagus nerve extends
deep into my body, slows my heart to swooning
when, for example, you touch my arm: my orbital
frontal cortex lights up like a neon *Vacancy*,
blinking invitation. Touch begets touch.
I feel the skin over your wrist, smooth
and cool and pulsing, so you pull me closer.
Neuropeptides flood my bloodstream. Scientists
can isolate the biological basis
of our connection, deeper than skin, chemicals
reacting, self-perpetuating like fire:
your touch, this calming, steady, burning breath.

# 2.

The chemistry is conclusive: when you leave,
my Pacinian corpuscles bend and falter.
My heart rate quickens; cortisol increases:
fight or flight? You are gone and there is no place
to which I wish to flee without you. My skin
loses heat, but the constancy of my circulation
suggests this longing is not fatal; your absence
leaves no scars; science is designed to protect us,
yet when you come back your fingers find
my skin less receptive, my oxytocin
slower to spread through my system, my shoulder cold
and turned against you. For days I might resist
your touch, though desire, like biology, is inevitable,
and I, predictably human, want always more.

# LOVE STORY

I planned to pierce his boil
with a surgeon's expert grace,
to slice the ugliness
erupting on his face;

I googled *inflamed blemish,*
*carbuncular infection,*
and sterilized a needle
with novice circumspection —

(that swelling contamination
has a subtle origin:
a foreign body roiling
deep beneath the skin) —

but poised before the abscess,
I paused and shrank, faint-hearted,
so he snatched the lance from me
and finished what I'd started.

When I asked him if it hurt,
his answer was unspoken:
alone we try to fix
what we ourselves have broken.

# LAST ANNIVERSARY

Nothingness, as far as we can understand,
implies emptiness, absence, an open hand

waiting for an offering to compensate
our deficiencies, an existential state

of mind, a vacant room; but no space to fill
existed, no time to kill, no weight until

the Big Bang gave us context, relativity,
the nothing we now know so well: proximity

defined by distance, existence a series
of contradictions born of complex theories.

Your expanding silence is a letter kept
but never opened. When we were young we slept

together in a single bed, my face
pressed in your neck, but now I need more space.

As if my body is a universe,
I reenact the Big Bang in reverse,

fetal, folding inward, longing to go back
to when "nothing" wasn't empty, silent, black:

no bodies to grow older, no hope to lose,
no desire, no indifference, no doors to close.

# MAXWELL'S DEMON

*"By dint of his prodigious intelligence and dexterity, the goblin could cause things to happen that are never seen to occur in nature, things that seemed able to violate the second law of thermodynamics." – Hans Christian von Baeyer*

Maxwell's demon, diminutive imp, you spit
on the law of entropy through the fork in your thick,
black tongue. You claw open trapdoors of closed systems,
let heat pass through, shut out the cold. Your lies
could keep my coffee hot all day. You want
to hold the hands of the clock steady, hold
gravity in check, unsag my skin, change

the nature of my longing, but even you
cannot exist without consequence: your gaze
alone alters everything you see. Like mine,
your presence interferes, unbalances, warps:
rubbernecking backs traffic up for miles, slows
the ambulance's progress, causes fender benders,
arguments, missed appointments, backseat births.

My weeping can't reverse a bullet, but
my limbic system shifts; the scent of day-old
lilies fills me, henceforth, with a sense of dread.
Darling liar, you promise endless heat,
backwards motion, do-overs. This time I know
exactly what to say. I *will* pick up
the phone this time. This time I'll tell him, *Wait.*

# MEDITATION ON DIVORCE DURING SUMMER STORM

The ice in my glass clinks lullaby as blackout
burns through our candlesticks. Thunder, a promise
kept, brings rainfall that saves me watering.

We watch drops play chase down windows of the house.
They plink against the shingles like grains of rice
spilling on a kitchen floor. Carelessness stalks

us all. A broken bird might fly again,
but his bent wing will spin him in circles.
We've been over this before, but the ground

is not, in fact, the same. What we forget
is that earth falls away; erosion gives
nothing back. Rain stops without a warning.

Our son, throughout this storm, has been dreaming hard
of lavender pressed between pages of a book
or river rocks that weigh his pockets down.

How are we to reckon this? A passing train
flattens our pennies into copper dots.
Tomorrow, we will find them scattered near

the tracks. The train tears through the night, Doppler's
warped frequencies like someone's forced goodbye.
Then comes calm, silence like a broken vow.

# BOTTOM DWELLERS

Nothing is wasted here: carcass of whale
feeds whole systems for decades; nothing is left

to rot: rattail fish and sleeper sharks tear
into the flesh; hagfish burrow deep,

consuming from within; mollusks lick clean
the bones; snails leach the mud. So scarce is food,

some creatures root themselves in sediment,
wait with open mouths to catch dead particles

that fall like snow. So scarce is light, their eyes
grow large with longing; some become invisible;

some bioluminesce, their organs throbbing
blue and green. For millions of years they have skulked

the abyssal plain, motherless and hungry.
Miles above, ships sail. My son points from the beach,

naming them all: container ship, yacht, trawler.
With pail and shovel he crouches, collecting

sand crabs and sea shells. Life spills over edges:
ocean into sand, sand into ocean,

this splashing, oblivious existence.
Now he gathers seaweed, bandaging himself

with the slippery strips. Now he shakes himself free,
runs along the shoreline, shouting at gulls.

Now he calls to me, pulls me away from questions
of open systems, delicate ecologies,

impossible depths, the mystery of adaptation:
life existing without language or light.

# HAVOC

More than wreaking havoc, chaos dictates
how time moves, just as seasons remind us how

we've changed. Last time the buds swelled up like broken
thumbs, last time the door shut, I bit my tongue.

I miss him as I miss my youthful haunts,
leveled years ago to make room for parking

and thoroughfares. I miss him the way I miss
my former self, captured in snapshot: unmasked

happiness. The sky was crossed with branches,
until spring brought a tapestry of green to hide

the river: chlorophyll glow in morning sun.
I am waking up alone again and find

that time is measured in the breaths I catch
while trying to stay calm. That Ken-doll hair,

those fingertips, insatiable thirst for me
and booze and late-night ramblings. Beginnings

are marked by openings: birth is the obvious
example, but also blossoms, windows, eyes.

The whole world opens with a first kiss,
but all that closes with a kiss goodbye

is a chapter in an imaginary book,
or maybe a literal door. Disaster's not

inherent in this course, but the onset
of turbulence breeds catastrophe: vortex

swirling into eddies, motion swift and
unpredictable. Chaos wreaks nothing

but time. It is we with our constant chatter,
our endless questions, who wreak havoc, we

with our need to narrate, fit events to plot,
who find ourselves misunderstanding, who

disorder the world around us. Always there's
wreckage. If you sit outside as we did,

early in spring, you can see the buds bursting,
leaves unfurling like a dress unfastened.

Separations are born of words we can't take back.
I hold my secrets close as unborn children.

My son is in love with the world and all it hides.
A robins' nest is tucked in a crumbling wall.

The robins come and go. The broken eggshell
can only mean two things: a beginning or

an end. There are too many variables
to measure who we are, and I'm not the girl

he thought I was. Chaos teaches infinity
and motion. Time moves and we are swept away.

I love him as I love the greening trees,
the river I no longer see. He can't

hear me, but I speak anyway. Words reach
a final line, this place where I can breathe.